BIRMINGHAM
a history of the city and its people

Malcolm Dick

Acknowledgements

Many people have contributed to this history and provided advice during its creation. The book originated within Birmingham Libraries and Information Services. I welcomed Martin Flynn's guidance during its early stages and Brian Gambles' management of the whole project. I would like to thank Alan Mahar of Tindal Street Press and Helen O'Brien of Birmingham Library Services for their support and editorial advice during the writing of this book. I am also grateful to Peter Leather and Alison Gove-Humphries for their corrections and suggestions. Other individuals, librarians, pupils and teachers, commented on the text, captions and illustrations. I am, of course, responsible for any errors which remain.

Local Studies and History at Birmingham Central Library, Birmingham City Archives and Birmingham Museums & Art Gallery provided many of the illustrations. Richard Albutt dealt efficiently with my requests for scanned images. I greatly appreciated the contributions by several photographers, including Sukhjinder Singh Kharaud, Peter Leather, Gareth Lewis, Barbara Palmer, Anthony Spettigue, Sukhvinder Singh Ubhi and Jim Warren. I would particularly like to thank Jim Warren for his lively and imaginative page design.

My work owes much to the writing of scholars, past and present, from William Hutton onwards. Their contributions to the narrative of this city will be recognisable from the pages of this book. Two projects — The Millennibrum Project from 2000 to 2002 and the Revolutionary Players Project from 2002 to 2004 — stimulated my interest in the history of this unique city. This interest has been sharpened by the enthusiasm of students at the University of Birmingham. I hope this book will likewise encourage children, their teachers and other readers to explore the past and present of this fascinating city.

First published October 2005
by Birmingham Library Services

CIP catalogue record for this book is available from the British Library.

ISBN Paperback 0 7093024 9 5
ISBN Hardback 0 7093025 4 1

Published by Birmingham Library Services
Designed by Jim Warren
Printed by Brewin Books, Studley, Warks
Project Management: Alan Mahar, Tindal Street Press
Editorial Support: Alan Mahar and Helen O'Brien, Centre for the Child
Copy-editing: Emma Hargrave, Tindal Street Press

Contents

Chapter 1
THE BEGINNINGS

The First Settlement

Birmingham is the most important English city after London. Its one million inhabitants come from all over the world, making it home to people of different cultures and faiths. It took hundreds of years for Birmingham to develop into such a large, diverse city.

Over 3,000 years ago the Birmingham area was home to people who created 'burnt mounds' of stones which archaeologists believe were either cooking sites or saunas. After this the Romans came when they invaded Britain in 43 AD. They built roads and a fort at Metchley in Edgbaston. In about 700 AD Anglo-Saxon tribes, who were originally from Germany, settled in the Midlands and gave Birmingham its name. 'Birmingham' is made up of three Anglo-Saxon words:

Brem or Beorma – the name of a person
ingas – descendants
ham – home

So, Birmingham means 'the home of the descendants of a leader or head of a family called Beorma'. Unfortunately, we do not know exactly where this settlement or 'home' was located.

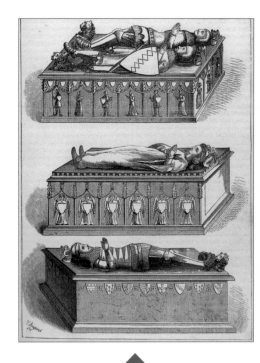

Monuments to the de Birmingham family in St Martin's Church

The Manor House of the de Birmingham family shortly before its demolition in 1815 to create Smithfield Market. The spire of St Martin's Church is in the background

Bermingeham, Brummagem and Brummies

The first description of Birmingham is in William the Conqueror's Domesday Book of 1086. At that time it was a poor farming district where about one hundred people lived. Nearby places such as Aston, Handsworth and King's Norton were richer and larger, but it was Birmingham which absorbed these settlements in later years and not the other way round. The modern spelling of Birmingham was not widely used until after 1700. In the Domesday Book Birmingham is written as 'Bermingeham', and there are over one hundred different versions of the city's name in later documents. When the word was spoken, people pronounced it as Brummagem or Bromicham and that is why people who live in the city are called Brummies.

The First Market and the Growth of Birmingham

Nothing in the Domesday Book suggested that Birmingham would become a major town. The big change began in 1166 when the lord of the manor, Peter de Birmingham, first gained permission from the king to hold a market, where Smithfield Market is today. The River Rea could be crossed nearby so it made sense for traders to use that site to buy and sell goods. The market brought newcomers, including Welsh people who sold cattle and sheep. They were the town's first minority community and they spoke their own language, Welsh.

Local industries developed. Cattle provided skins for leather work. Carts pulled by animals brought iron for metal work and coal for fuel from the Black Country. Clay was made into pottery. Springs and streams provided water for washing and dyeing cloth and for cleaning animal hides.

In the early 1300s Birmingham had about 1,000 inhabitants and became the third largest town in Warwickshire after Coventry and Warwick. But fourteenth-century Birmingham, like other places in England, was hit by bad weather, crop failure and plagues, such as the Black Death from 1348 to 1350. The number of people living in Birmingham declined until it rose again in the fifteenth century.

St Martin's Church is the only surviving building from these times in central Birmingham. Not much remains from the twelfth- and thirteenth-century church as it was completely rebuilt in the nineteenth century.

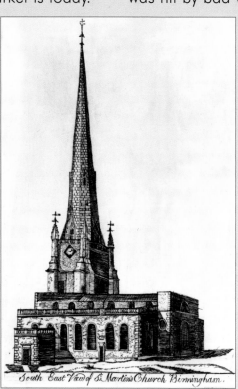

South East View of St Martin's Church Birmingham.

Builders have altered St Martin's Church many times during the centuries. This picture dates from the eighteenth century

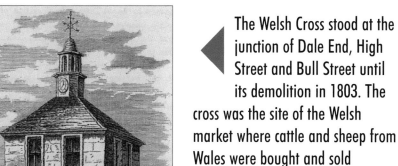

The Welsh Cross stood at the junction of Dale End, High Street and Bull Street until its demolition in 1803. The cross was the site of the Welsh market where cattle and sheep from Wales were bought and sold

This is how the area around St Martin's looks today

Chapter 2

The Noise of Anvils

Birmingham had about 1,500 inhabitants in 1500. By 1700 its population had grown rapidly to about 8,000, making it the fourteenth largest town in Britain. John Leland was a visitor to the town in 1538. He journeyed through Deritend, over the River Rea and past St Martin's Church, and described the making of knives, bits for horses and nails in the town.

In 1563 another traveller, William Camden, found Birmingham 'swarming with inhabitants and echoing with the noise of Anvils'. The anvils were worked by blacksmiths who needed a bellows, hammers and various tools as well as an

Birmingham, in 1640, viewed from the south. A cluster of buildings stretches from the River Rea in the foreground to St Martin's Church at the top of the picture (Dugdale's Antiquities of Warwickshire, 1656)

anvil to set up in business. They made nails and other goods out of iron and worked in forges with their living accommodation on top.

Camden also described Birmingham's appearance. The lower part of the town was 'very watery', but the upper part, around New Street and High Street, 'rises with abundance of handsome buildings'. As a busy,

prosperous town, Birmingham was home to wealthy men and women who profited from its growth. Among them was the Colmore family, who gave their name to Colmore Row, and the Smalbrokes after whom Smallbrook Queensway is named.

This photograph of a blacksmith with his anvil dates from 1920. In the sixteenth century there were very many blacksmiths living and working in Birmingham

rich enough to build Blakesley Hall in Yardley in 1590. It was a large modern house with fireplaces, brick chimneys and glass in the windows.

Barbara Smalbroke (1593–1679) was the daughter of Robert Smalbroke, the son of the second Richard Smalbroke. She died when she was eighty-six years old at a time when most women died before they were forty. Her father died when she was ten and she inherited Blakesley Hall in 1613 on the death of her grandfather. A prosperous woman, she was married twice, to the sons of local landowners. Her first husband died after two years of marriage, but in 1620 Barbara married Aylmer Foliot of Perton Court in Pershore, with whom she had fourteen children.

▲ Blakesley Hall is now a museum of seventeenth-century life.

The Smalbroke Family and Blakesley Hall

Richard Smalbroke made a big impact on the sixteenth-century town. He owned land in Yardley and sold cloth, spices, groceries and metal goods in Birmingham. In 1536 King Henry VIII took away most of the land which belonged to the Church and sold it to wealthy individuals. Smalbroke acquired some of the Church's property in the town, including the Old Crown in Deritend. He also became one of the first governors of Edward VI Grammar School, which was built in New Street. Richard's son, also called Richard, was

An open-fronted forge with living accommodation on top

Forges and Flintlocks

Not everyone was as wealthy as the Smalbrokes. Most people made their living by working with their hands. In 1683 Birmingham had around two hundred forges, where nails, tools and swords were manufactured from iron and steel. Brass making was another local industry. Candlesticks, pots and weights were all made out of brass. The manufacture of flintlocks started in the seventeenth century. Flintlocks were rifles which used the sparks from striking flints to ignite gunpowder to fire a lead ball. Birmingham's long involvement in gun making started during the Civil War.

The Battle of Birmingham

Local weapons were in high demand during the Civil War which lasted from 1642 to 1651. This war was caused by a struggle between King Charles I, who was head of the Church of England, and Parliament which was supported by the Puritans who opposed the King and Church. Local preachers, such as Thomas Hall from Kings Norton, John Burgess in Sutton Coldfield and Francis Roberts at St Martin's, attacked King Charles and the Church of England in spoken words and in print from their pulpits.

When the Civil War started, many guns and swords made in Birmingham were supplied to the Parliamentary Army. This angered the Royalists, who supported Charles. On Easter Monday 1643 the King's nephew, Prince Rupert, led a force of 2,000 men to punish the people of Birmingham for supplying the King's enemies with weapons. The town had no wall to defend it from invaders, so the Prince's troops entered easily. In the 'Battle of Birmingham' they forced their way into people's homes where they stole property and terrified women and children. This attack on ordinary citizens made Birmingham people suspicious of those in power for a long time afterwards.

▲ This picture in an anti-royalist pamphlet shows Prince Rupert at the Battle of Birmingham. Rupert is firing his pistol and Birmingham is burning behind him

▲ The Grammar School, King's Norton

Thomas Hall, King's Norton Grammar School and the Puritans

Thomas Hall (1610–1665) was master of the grammar school in King's Norton and a Puritan preacher. He was a hard-working and very strict teacher and a strong supporter of Parliament in the Civil War. During his career he published many books. One was on the 'loathsomeness of long hair' and another attacked the use of make-up by women who spent their time 'painting, patching, spotting and blotting themselves'. Hall lost his job in 1662 after Charles II, the son of Charles I, became king. He died in poverty and was buried in King's Norton churchyard. The grammar school building where he taught still survives and his impressive library of books is kept at Birmingham Central Library.

Thomas Holte, Aston Hall and the Royalists

Aston Hall is one of the few surviving seventeenth-century buildings in Birmingham which played a part in the Civil War. It was built by Sir Thomas Holte (1571–1654) on high ground overlooking the road from Birmingham to Lichfield. The Holtes were rich and influential landowners, and Aston Hall became a grand palace to show how powerful they were. Sir Thomas used iron slag or waste from his iron works to create the foundations, and the hall was built from local clay bricks and sandstone. It took seventeen years to complete and was finished in 1635.

A picture imagining the damage caused to the staircase at Aston Hall during the Civil War

 Nineteenth-century view of Aston Hall

Sir Thomas Holte supported the Royalists, and in 1642 King Charles I spent the night at Aston Hall before the nearby Battle of Edgehill which began the Civil War. In 1643 the Hall was attacked by the Parliamentary Army. Evidence of this can still be seen in the damaged staircase on Aston Hall's first floor landing.

Aston Hall today

Chapter 4

PEOPLE AND PLACES

A Rapidly Growing Town

Birmingham was the fastest-growing town in eighteenth-century Britain. 15,000 people lived there in 1730 and by 1801 the number had grown to 73,670. More and more people came to Birmingham from elsewhere in England, Ireland, Scotland and Wales. Jewish refugees from Europe and black people from Africa and the West Indies also lived in the town. Birmingham became a place of many communities and different beliefs. There were members of the Church of England (Anglicans), Jews, Quakers, Roman Catholics, Unitarians and those who had no religious faith. This diversity contributed to the development of Birmingham as a creative, dynamic and forward-looking town.

St Philip's Church: the Local Landmark

In the eighteenth century Birmingham's civic pride was represented by St Philip's Church, now Birmingham's Anglican Cathedral in Colmore Row. It was designed by Thomas Archer (1668/9–1743), and built in 1725 to serve the area around High Street and New Street. St Philip's dominated the local landscape from its hill-top site. William Hutton (1723–1815), Birmingham's first historian, arrived in the town from Derby in 1741 and was amazed by the 'superb edifice', which was 'untarnished by smoke, and illuminated by the western sun'. St Philip's is still one of Birmingham's most beautiful buildings, but nowadays it is dominated by the newer and taller buildings which surround it.

 St Philip's Church, now Birmingham's Anglican Cathedral

John Ash and the General Hospital

There was no National Health Service in the eighteenth century. Wealthy people were treated at home, but the poor had to rely on folk medicine or the charity of doctors. In 1765 a local doctor, John Ash (1722–1789), who came from Coventry, began raising money for a free hospital in Birmingham to treat poor people. Local residents donated money and organised music festivals to raise funds.

In 1779, 170 years before the start of the NHS, Birmingham's General Hospital admitted its first patients.

1774 oil painting of John Baskerville by James Millar, a Birmingham artist (Birmingham Museums and Art Gallery)

John Baskerville: 'Man of Genius'

At this time most people believed in God, but John Baskerville (1706–1775) was an exception. He was an atheist and said that when he died he would not be buried in a churchyard. Instead he was buried upright in a coffin near his own house. Baskerville came to Birmingham from Worcestershire as a boy. He carved stone, taught writing and in 1757 he set up a printing business which made a great difference to how books were produced. Today we use computers to produce printed material, but in the eighteenth century text was printed from lead type which was spread with ink and pressed onto paper. Early eighteenth-century books were difficult to read: letters were close together and the ink was grey rather than black. Baskerville invented a new font – a style of lettering – which was named after him, and he developed a deep-black printing ink. He printed beautiful books of poetry and copies of the Bible which were easy to read. Baskerville wanted ordinary people to discover knowledge for themselves and not be influenced by superstition or the opinions of people in authority. His books made Birmingham into a town where reading, thinking and questioning flourished.

A monument to the Baskerville font outside Baskerville House in Centenary Square

In 1758 Baskerville became Printer to the University of Cambridge and was able to achieve his ambition to publish a Bible. His bold designs were made more striking by using deep-black ink on special paper which was pressed between hot copper plates. 1,250 copies of his 1763 Bible were printed.

This title page is from a Baskerville Bible at St Philip's Cathedral in Birmingham

Chapter 5

INDUSTRY AND CANALS

The Brass House was built in 1781 to manufacture brass in Birmingham and avoid the need to transport the raw metal alloy from elsewhere

Brass and the Brass House

During the eighteenth century, Birmingham changed from a small manufacturing centre into the most important industrial town in Britain. The brass trade was one of Birmingham's industries. For most of the century local manufacturers made brass buckles, buttons and horse and carriage fittings from brass which was made outside the town. In 1781 a rise in the price of the metal made Birmingham businessmen try a new approach. The Birmingham Metal Company was set up and the Brass House built on Broad Street so that the industry no longer had to rely on expensive imports. By 1800 Birmingham was Britain's centre for brass making. The trade has left its mark on the way we speak. We get down to 'brass tacks' when we mean business, our bosses are 'top brass' and we might be 'brassed off' by boring work.

Canals and Coal

Eighteenth-century roads were narrow and easily damaged by the carts which moved heavy goods such as coal and iron into Birmingham. They also transported manufactured goods to markets elsewhere. Industrialists like Matthew Boulton (1728–1809) encouraged the building of canals to serve their needs. In 1769 the engineer James Brindley (1716–1772) constructed a canal between Birmingham and the coal mines in Wednesbury. Cheaper transport costs meant that the price of coal went down. More canals were built over the next sixty years linking Birmingham to the Rivers Trent, Severn, Mersey and Thames, and to the ports of Hull, Bristol, Liverpool and London.

Nineteenth- and twentieth-century buildings along the canal in Gas Street Basin

Matthew Boulton: Industrial Pioneer

Matthew Boulton was the son of a local manufacturer of buttons and buckles. In 1745 he entered his father's business. Between 1756 and 1761 he used Sarehole Mill, now a museum in Hall Green, to produce sheet metal using water power. In 1762 he opened the Soho Works in Handsworth, where silver candlesticks, dishes, spoons and forks were made. Boulton employed talented designers to create his products, set up a marketing section at the Soho Works and sent out agents to learn the industrial secrets of other nations. By 1800 the Soho Works was the largest factory in the world.

Oil painting of Matthew Boulton at 42, by JSC Schaak, 1770 (Soho House Museum, Birmingham)

Sarehole Mill today

The quality of gold and silver objects is shown by a 'hallmark' stamped into the metal to guard against forgery. This stamping is done at an assay office. Boulton grew tired of sending his goods away to the Assay Office at Chester and he tried to persuade Parliament to set up an office in Birmingham. In 1773 he succeeded. The Assay Office contributed to Birmingham's reputation as a producer of high quality silverware and jewellery. The Assay Office still exists to control the quality of local silverware.

Branched and ornamental candlesticks made by Matthew Boulton and his business partner, John Fothergill, in about 1775 (Soho House Museum, Birmingham)

In 1775 Boulton and the Scots inventor, James Watt, began to manufacture Watt's steam pump and in 1795 the Soho Foundry in Smethwick was built. It was the first factory to produce steam engines. Boulton also developed ways of making coins more difficult to counterfeit. By the time of his death in 1809, Boulton, together with other local industrialists, had turned Birmingham into Britain's most significant centre for making metal goods, steam engines and machinery. It became known as the town of a 'thousand trades'.

Chapter 6
THE LUNAR SOCIETY

The Face of the Moon, by John Russell, c.1795 (Soho House Museum, Birmingham). The artist looked at the moon through a telescope and created this pastel drawing from chalk mixed with other materials. Astronomy was one of the interests of the Lunar Society

The Lunar Society: Thinkers and Practical Men

Birmingham's industrial development was also encouraged by members of the Lunar Society. They were writers, scientists, inventors and businessmen who met at one another's homes in and around Birmingham whenever there was a full moon. Their meetings began in 1765 when Dr William Small (1734–1775) moved to Birmingham after teaching in the British colony of Virginia, now part of the USA. He helped to bring these multi-talented people together.

What did the Lunar Men do? They:

- built factories and canals throughout the Midlands
- invented new machines such as the steam engine
- experimented with gases, minerals and chemicals to improve the pottery, glass and metal industries
- increased our knowledge of geology, electricity, engineering and medicine
- influenced politics, religion and education
- were involved in the anti-slavery campaign.

Who were the Lunar Men?

Name	Dates	Homes at the time of the Lunar Society	Activities
Matthew Boulton	1728–1809	Birmingham and Handsworth	Industrialist
Erasmus Darwin	1731–1802	Lichfield and Derby	Doctor, Writer
Thomas Day	1748–1789	Lichfield and Southern England	Writer, Reformer
Richard Lovell Edgeworth	1744–1817	Lichfield, Southern England and Ireland	Inventor, Reformer
Samuel Galton Jnr	1753–1832	Birmingham	Industrialist
James Keir	1735–1820	West Bromwich	Inventor
Joseph Priestley	1733–1804	Birmingham	Scientist, Reformer
William Small	1734–1775	Birmingham	Inventor, Doctor
James Watt	1736–1819	Handsworth	Inventor
Josiah Wedgwood	1730–1795	North Staffordshire	Industrialist
John Whitehurst	1713–1788	Derby and London	Geologist, Engineer
William Withering	1741–1799	Edgbaston	Doctor

The Society's Meeting Place: Soho House

Matthew Boulton's house in Soho, Handsworth, was where many Lunar Society meetings were held. Soho House was a very modern home for the eighteenth century. Boulton installed coal-fired central heating, which was almost unknown at the time, and an observatory where he could investigate the moon, planets and stars through a telescope. Soho House was near an inn which had links with fox hunting. The name 'so-ho' is thought to derive from the sound made by a hunting horn.

◄ In 1761 Matthew Boulton bought Soho Mill and House on Handsworth Heath. He created a huge factory at the mill and made alterations to his home. Boulton moved into Soho House with his wife, Ann, in 1766. In the 1790s the building was re-designed inside and out by Samuel and James Wyatt. When it was built Soho House was in the countryside, but it is now part of Handsworth

A Medical Discovery: Digitalis

In 1775, when William Small died, the Lunar Society invited Dr William Withering (1741–1799) to join the group. Withering had studied how the drug digitalis, from the foxglove plant, affected the heart. In the eighteenth century, heart problems were treated with foxglove leaves, but people did not know what quantities to use or how to prevent side effects such as headaches and vomiting. Withering discovered how much digitalis should be given to sick people by carefully measuring the doses and the effects they had on his patients. He wrote a book describing his experiments. By working in this way Withering became one of the founders of modern medicine. Digitalis is still used today to treat heart disease.

Foxglove illustration from William Withering's 'An Account of the Foxglove and Some of its Medical Uses', published in 1795 (Birmingham Central Library)

The End of the Lunar Society

What happened to the Lunar Society? During riots in 1791 a mob destroyed Joseph Priestley's house, laboratory and library because he supported the revolution in France against the monarchy and he also wanted greater democracy and human rights in Britain. Priestley fled to London and then left to live as a refugee in the USA. The Lunar Society started to meet less often and meetings ended altogether in the early 1800s, but the scientific, technological and medical activities of the Lunar men have had a lasting influence on today's world.

Chapter 7
THE ANTI-SLAVERY CAMPAIGN

The Lunar Men and Anti-slavery

Part of Birmingham's wealth came from the chains and guns which were made in the town. These were sold in Africa to buy slaves and used to control them on West Indian sugar plantations. Some people willingly made their money from selling chains and guns, but many local people, including members of the Lunar Society, protested against the slave trade and slavery because they were horrified at how slaves were treated. Campaigners wore badges designed by Josiah Wedgwood (1730–1795) and refused to eat sugar produced by slaves. In 1788 Joseph Priestley (1733–1804) preached and published a sermon in Birmingham to encourage local people to sign a petition to Parliament. He described slavery as 'the greatest, and most crying evil under the sun'. All human beings, he said, were neighbours, whether they lived in Asia, Africa or America, were Christians, Jews or Muslims, or belonged to another religion. If people were suffering 'we ought . . . to relieve their distresses', he told his audience.

'Am I not a Man and a Brother' was designed by Josiah Wedgwood in 1787. Opponents of slavery wore this image on buttons, brooches and bracelets

Sometimes a slave owner borrowed money and could not pay it back. As slaves were his property they could be sold to pay his debts. This could lead to the separation of mothers, fathers and children. Anti-slavery campaigners used this picture to show how slavery caused human suffering

Equiano's Visit to Birmingham

One anti-slavery campaigner who came to Birmingham was a former slave, Olaudah Equiano (1745–1797). In 1789 he published his autobiography, *An Interesting Narrative*, which became a best-selling book. It was the most important eighteenth-century account of the slave trade and slavery by a Black British writer.

At the age of ten, in about 1755, Equiano was kidnapped from his home in West Africa. He was imprisoned on board an English ship and transported to the Caribbean where he was sold into slavery. Equiano spent the next ten years of his life in Virginia, England and the West Indies, but he gained his freedom in 1766. Once free he became a successful trader.

Equiano came to Birmingham in 1790 to help sell his book. In a letter to the newspaper, *Aris's Birmingham Gazette*, he thanked people for their kindness, hospitality and 'fellow-feeling' towards 'my very poor and oppressed countrymen'. He looked forward to a time when he could entertain his Birmingham friends with the best foods that Africa produced, including pineapples and palm wine.

Portrait of Olaudah Equiano from his autobiography

Women and Anti-slavery

In 1807 Parliament abolished the slave trade. This stopped Africans being taken from their homes and being sold into slavery in the British Empire, but slavery continued to exist in the West Indies. The Female Society for the Relief of British Negro Slaves, which was formed in 1825, was an anti-slavery organisation supported by women in the Birmingham area. It held meetings and published anti-slavery poems and pictures. Mary Anne Galton (1778–1856), the daughter of Samuel Galton Jnr was a member. Her father sold guns which were exchanged for slaves in Africa. As a girl Mary Anne refused to eat West Indian sugar to protest against slave labour on sugar plantations.

Slavery in the British Empire was abolished in the 1830s, but campaigners such as the Female Society and Quaker abolitionist, Joseph Sturge (1793–1859), continued to champion free labour and to oppose slavery throughout the world. Sturge's statue can still be seen at Five Ways

I would not have a Slave to till my ground
To carry me, to fan me while I sleep,
And tremble when I wake, for all the wealth
That sinews bought and sold have ever earn'd.
We have no Slaves at home—why then abroad?

COWPER.

The Female Society used this picture and poem to draw attention to the mental and physical suffering of slaves

The Welsh and Scots: Businessmen, Singers and Sportsmen

Most migrants came from nearby counties such as Worcestershire, Staffordshire and Shropshire, but others travelled from Wales, Scotland and Ireland.

Sampson Lloyd (1664–1724) arrived from Wales in 1698. His family set up iron works in Birmingham and gave their name to what is now Lloyd's TSB. In the 1830s Welshmen helped to build the Town Hall and their male-voice choirs contributed to local musical life.

Scottish newcomers included James Watt and his engineers, James Lawson and Gilbert Hamilton.

Football also owes a great deal to Scotsmen who moved south. In 1874 Aston Villa was founded by George Ramsay, a clerk in the brass industry, and financed by George Kynoch, the industrialist. William McGregor, a local Scottish merchant, was one of the founders of the Football League in 1888.

 'Farm', Sparkbrook, the home of the Lloyd family, was built in the 1740s

William Murdock

William Murdock: Scottish Engineer

In 1777 William Murdock (1754–1839) left his home in Scotland and walked hundreds of miles to Handsworth to fulfil his dream of working on James Watt's steam engine. He was a trained engineer, and Boulton and Watt employed him in their Soho Works. Murdock improved Watt's engine and used coal gas to produce light. In 1802 he created a gas light display outside the Soho factory to celebrate the end of the war with France.

The Irish: Builders of Birmingham

Irish people fled poverty in Ireland to find work. They contributed to Birmingham by building factories, roads and railways. According to a medical report in 1828, many of the Irish emigrants faced poverty in Birmingham: 'They become mason's labourers, or follow whatever other casual occupations they can obtain. They are badly clothed, miserably fed, and miserably lodged, and in every respect exhibit a striking contrast to their more fortunate neighbours.'

Most Irish people were Roman Catholics. Birmingham's first Irish priest, Thomas M McDonnell, was a leading campaigner in the 1820s to give more people the right to vote. St Chad's Cathedral was built in 1841 as a place of worship for Catholic communities in Birmingham.

St Chad's Cathedral. Designed by Augustus Pugin, it is considered to be one of the most beautiful neo-gothic churches in the UK

John Frederick Feeney: Journalist and Newspaper Owner

One man from Ireland, John Frederick Feeney (1807–1869), created two of today's local newspapers: *The Birmingham Post* and *Evening Mail*. He learned the printing trade in Ireland and came to Birmingham in 1835 to edit a weekly anti-slavery paper, *The Philanthropist*. When slavery ended in the British Empire in 1838 the need for the paper disappeared. Feeney looked for a new role. He bought an existing paper, *The Birmingham Journal*, in 1844 and increased its daily sales from 1,200 to 23,000 by 1857. In the same year he created a cheaper paper, *The Birmingham Daily Post*, which was sold across the West Midlands to farmers, manufacturers and traders. Speed was vital. Feeney used the electric telegraph, an early form of teletext, to obtain information, and the railways to distribute his paper to readers. He also began the *Saturday Evening Post* to provide a summary of the week's news for ordinary readers. When Feeney died in 1869 the *Journal* closed down. His two other papers remain but now with slightly different names, *The Birmingham Post* and *Evening Mail*.

Chapter 9

INCOMERS FROM OVERSEAS

The Jewish Community

Birmingham's first refugees were Jewish people who fled persecution in Central Europe during the eighteenth century. They settled in Birmingham's poorest district, the Froggery, on the site of New Street Station, and earned a living by small-scale trading. They were prevented from owning land or entering the professions, but the leader of their synagogue, Rabbi Isaiah Phillips (1746–1834), encouraged his congregation to make contact with local people and give to Birmingham charities. In 1856 the Jewish community built a magnificent synagogue at Singers Hill, close to the Mailbox, which still survives today.

Nurse and child in Birmingham's Children's Hospital 1904. The bed was maintained by the 'Jewish Children's Guild of Kindness'

Singers Hill Synagogue today

Black Christians

Black people also lived in eighteenth-century Birmingham, but we know little about the detail of their lives. The records of St Martin's Church name individuals who were baptised or buried in the town. In 1887 the Reverend Peter Stanford came to Birmingham. He became a pastor in local Baptist churches, including the Wilberforce Memorial Church on Priestley Road. Stanford wrote an autobiography, *From Bondage to Liberty*, and an account of black people in the USA, *The Tragedy of the Negro in America*. Stanford loved Birmingham and described leaving 'my Birmingham Church' for America as 'the greatest trial of my life because the kindness and love of many friends must be left behind'.

The Reverend Peter Stanford, who was born as a slave in the USA

Italian Craftsmen

Italians escaped the poverty of their homeland during the late nineteenth century and settled in Digbeth. St Michael's Church, where Irish Catholics also worshipped, was a centre for the Italian community. Some Italians created decorative marble floors for local buildings and others earned a living as factory workers, musicians, lodging-house keepers and ice-cream sellers.

Italian ice-cream seller in the Bull Ring, 1895

George Edalji: a Wrongly Accused Man

Birmingham was also home to Asian people. In 1869 Joseph Salter, a Christian missionary, noted that there were three lodging houses for Indians in the town. These men had probably been sailors who had left their ships to find better paid work in industry.

George Edalji (1876–1953) was a local Asian who made legal history. He was the son of an Indian Christian who married an English woman and became the vicar of Great Wyrley in Staffordshire. Some local people resented the presence of the family in the parish so they sent them threatening letters. George was a bright boy and went on to study law in Birmingham. In 1899 he began work as a local solicitor.

In 1903 the police received reports that farm animals in Great Wyrley were being injured, and George Edalji was blamed. He was arrested, tried, found guilty, sentenced to seven years in prison and forbidden to practise as a solicitor. Immediately a campaign began for his release and the government freed him, but without a pardon. He tried to clear his name and obtained the help of Arthur Conan Doyle, the author of the Sherlock Holmes stories. A government enquiry found George Edalji innocent of the crime of maiming animals, and he was given a free pardon and allowed to work as a solicitor again.

Some good came out of his ordeal: the Criminal Court of Appeal was created. This gives a second trial to people who have mistakenly been found guilty.

Chapter 10

WORKERS AND TRADES

The Health of Workers

Industrial workers in nineteenth-century Birmingham were better paid than workers elsewhere, but their work had a bad effect on their health. The town's young men were smaller than the national average. An army recruiting sergeant was reported to have said that: 'the mechanics are generally shorter than in any town he [had] known, the general height being from five feet four inches to five feet five inches.' Brassworkers had a short life span because their work was so dangerous. The fumes released during brass-making caused lung diseases and, in one district with many brass foundries, the 'green snow' produced by the foundries would fall on local residents.

The Brassworks of Messrs R W Winfield and Co., founded in 1829

The Jewellery Quarter

In the nineteenth century the Jewellery Quarter was a district of small workshops. Its history goes back to 1746 when part of the Colmore Estate was sold to businesses, which included button and buckle makers as well as jewellers. When gold was discovered in California and Australia in the mid-nineteenth century, sales of jewellery increased dramatically. By 1913 over 30,000 people were employed in the Quarter as silversmiths, ring makers and electroplaters. Today the Quarter has its own museum and Europe's best surviving group of jewellery workshops.

An example of a nineteenth-century workshop at the back of Great Hampton Street in the Jewellery Quarter

Jacob Jacobs: Reinventing the Jewellery Trade

Jacob Jacobs (1839–1896) was a member of the Jewish community. His father had moved from Sheffield in 1852 and became a jewellery trader in Vittoria Street. Young Jacobs grew up to become an energetic and creative businessman. In the 1880s sales of jewellery were in decline. Jacobs and other local businessmen invited HRH Alexandra, the Princess of Wales, to wear Birmingham jewellery to encourage other women to buy necklaces and brooches made in the town. The Princess accepted their invitation and demand increased. Jacobs formed the Birmingham Jewellers' and Silversmiths' Association in 1887. In 1890 it set up the Jewellers' Technical School where workers could improve their knowledge of the trade. It became the School of Jewellery and is now part of the University of Central England.

Jacobs also chaired a company which built the Great Western Arcade, opposite Snow Hill Station. This was a pedestrianised street lit by huge gas chandeliers where people could shop for luxury items sheltered from the weather. In the 1890s it was said to be the finest arcade in the world and it is still a shopping centre today.

The Great Western Arcade in the 1990s

The Gun Quarter

Most of Birmingham's Gun Quarter was demolished in the 1960s and 1970s, but a few examples of nineteenth-century workshops remain in the streets near St Chad's Cathedral. Skilled workers in small businesses made gun parts or assembled them into finished products. The quality of these guns was tested in the Birmingham Proof House, which still exists today. In the late nineteenth century the sale of mass-produced guns such as the Colt Revolver, from the USA, threatened the survival of the area. Small businesses could not compete and large companies were formed which could concentrate on mass production. These included Birmingham Small Arms (BSA), which was set up in Small Heath in 1861. BSA later became famous for making motorcycles.

A skilled gun maker at work in the late twentieth century. The tools he uses are very similar to those used in the nineteenth century

Chapter 11

FACTORIES AND RAILWAYS

Glass, Screws, Beer, Sauce and Custard

Most industrial goods were made in workshops in the nineteenth century, but factories gradually became more important. They included Chance Brothers, which created the glass for the Crystal Palace in London and lights for lighthouses, and Chamberlain and Nettlefolds, the largest screw-makers in Britain. Both were based in Smethwick, which is now part of Sandwell. Aston residents lived with the smell of beer from Ansells Brewery and vinegar from the Midland Vinegar Company. The latter started making HP Sauce in 1903. Alfred Bird invented egg-free custard powder in 1837. His company's custard factory in Digbeth is now a centre for the arts and small businesses.

▲ The Custard Factory today

The Birmingham Pen Trade

The manufacture of pens moved from workshops to factories in the nineteenth century. Most pens today are ball-point or felt-tip pens, but 200 years ago people used quill pens which were made from goose feathers. They had to be skilfully cut to create a point and they easily wore out. Pens were also made out of steel, but early steel pens were not flexible enough for comfortable writing and the steel was corroded by acid in the ink. The Birmingham steel pen trade, which developed in the 1820s, used Sheffield steel which was more flexible and resisted corrosion. New factories produced pens cheaply and in enormous quantities. 1,198,000,000 pens were made in the town by 1886. The varieties of pen included very fine pens for drawing maps and others with five nibs for creating the lines of music scores.

Grinding in Joseph Gillott and Sons, Pen Manufacturer ▼

Joseph Gillott and Pen Making

Joseph Gillott (1799–1872) pioneered factory production in pen making. He was born in Sheffield, where he first worked making steel knives. In 1822 he moved to Birmingham where he found work creating small metal items such as buckles and chains. One branch of this trade was the manufacture of steel pen nibs. The nibs had to be hand-made and were expensive to buy. Gillott developed a way of using machines to make pen nibs. His business expanded and in 1839 he moved into a large purpose-built factory, the Victoria Works in Graham Street in the Jewellery Quarter, a building which still exists today.

Gillott employed about 450 workers, mainly women, to manufacture nibs. The low cost of these steel pens meant that they were affordable to most people.

Joseph Gillott and Sons, Pen Manufacturer, Graham Street, Birmingham

Curzon Street and New Street Stations

Birmingham's railways developed to serve local workshops and factories. The Liverpool to Birmingham Railway, which was also known as the Grand Junction Railway, reached Vauxhall near Birmingham in 1837 and a year later the London to Birmingham Railway linked Euston Station with Curzon Street. By 1842 four railway companies operated from Curzon Street. But unfortunately it was too far from the centre of Birmingham. So, in 1854, New Street Station was opened so that passengers could arrive in and leave the centre of Birmingham by rail. When it was built it had the largest iron and glass roof in the world. In the 1960s the nineteenth-century station was demolished and replaced by a modern building.

The entrance to Curzon Street Station today. It is now home to the Royal College of Organists

Early twentieth-century photograph of the inside of New Street Station

New Markets and Buildings

Between 1750 and 1831 Birmingham's population grew from 24,000 to 146,986. This expansion created serious problems of pollution, overcrowding and crime. Before 1838 Birmingham had no town government, only parish councils and local courts. They had few powers and were unable to improve the environment in the growing town.

In 1769 Parliament set up a Board of Street Commissioners to clean and light the streets, remove public health dangers and redevelop the town centre. At that time Birmingham's market was crammed into the narrow streets around St Martin's Church. On market days there were traffic jams of carts, wagons and animals. The Commissioners cleared the medieval moat, demolished the wooden buildings around the church and removed the old market cross. They opened a large market space in the Bull Ring in 1806 and moved the cattle market. A courtroom, prison and public offices were opened in Moor Street in 1807. In the 1830s the Market Hall, which was destroyed by German bombs in 1940, and the Town Hall were built.

The Bull Ring Market in the 1820s. Nelson's statue is visible in front of St Martin's Church

Nelson's Statue in the 1970s. Since then his statue has been moved to the new Bullring

Birmingham's First Statue: Admiral Lord Nelson

Birmingham acquired its first public statue in 1809. It was of Admiral Lord Nelson (1758–1805), who made Britain into the world's most important sea power. The bronze statue replaced the market cross and provided a new feature in the Bull Ring, overlooking St Martin's Church. Birmingham is a long way from the sea, so it might seem strange that local people should give money to build a statue of an admiral. But Nelson was a national hero for his success in fighting the French. And in 1802 Nelson went to Birmingham, where he visited local factories and was kept awake at night by the cheering crowds outside his hotel wanting to see him. He died in 1805 at the Battle of Trafalgar.

The Town Hall: a Roman Temple in Birmingham

Until the International Convention Centre opened in 1991, the Town Hall in Victoria Square was the main venue for concerts, conferences and public meetings. In 1830 a competition was held to select a design to seat 3,000 people for music festivals. It was won by a young architect, Joseph Hansom, and his business partner, Edmund Welch. Hansom's design was in the style of a Roman temple with a brick structure faced with limestone from Anglesey in Wales. The building was opened in 1834, but not finished until 1849. The Town Hall was closed in the 1990s, but is now being refurbished.

 The Town Hall in 1991 before renovation

Thomas Attwood and the Vote

Nowadays almost all adults in Britain are allowed to vote in elections. This was not always the case. Only a small number of men and no women could vote in the early nineteenth century. In 1830 a local banker, Thomas Attwood (1783–1856), tried to change this by setting up a campaigning organisation, the Birmingham Political Union. Attwood lobbied Parliament to change the law. The First Reform Act (1832) allowed more men to vote and enabled big towns such as Birmingham to choose their own MPs for the first time. Attwood became an MP for Birmingham.

Nineteenth-century portrait of Thomas Attwood

Chapter 13

JOSEPH CHAMBERLAIN

Manufacturer, Mayor and Minister

Joseph Chamberlain (1836–1914) was born in London and moved to Birmingham to help run the family firm of Nettlefold and Chamberlain. He was interested in politics as well as business. Chamberlain wanted to provide schools for the children of Birmingham's workers and to increase the number of men who could vote. He was Mayor from 1873 to 1876, and in 1876 he was elected as a Liberal MP for Birmingham. Chamberlain went on to become a minister in both Liberal and Conservative governments. He also helped to set up the University of Birmingham in 1900. Chamberlain Square and Highbury Hall are reminders of his contribution to the area.

Portrait of Joseph Chamberlain

The Corporation and the Council House

Between 1841 and 1901, the population of Birmingham rose from 182,922 to 522,204. At the same time local government also expanded. In 1838 the town acquired an elected corporation, or council, led by a mayor. In 1851 it took over the work of the Street Commissioners. The Corporation improved the water supply and laid down tramways for public transport. In 1871 a competition was held to design a new Council House in Victoria Square. In 1870 the designs of Yeoville Thomason were selected and construction began in 1874.

In 1889 Queen Victoria granted Birmingham city status, which recognised its importance as one of Britain's great towns. Its successful management of local services meant it was described as the 'best-governed city in the world'. As Birmingham's mayor in the 1870s Joseph Chamberlain transformed the delivery of services to local people.

The statue of Joseph Priestley surveys Chamberlain Square and the Chamberlain monument, outside the Museum and Art Gallery

Highbury Hall, Moseley, the home of Joseph Chamberlain

The Civic Gospel: a Christian Approach to the Local Community

Chamberlain was influenced by George Dawson (1821–1876), a Christian clergyman who preached what became known as the 'Civic Gospel'. He believed that local councils had a religious duty to look after the welfare of poor people and to improve the local environment. Good sewerage and water supply reduced diseases caused by bad drains and polluted drinking water. Street crimes such as muggings were less likely in well-lit streets. Parks, libraries, schools, museums and art galleries gave everyone the same opportunities to exercise and improve their minds.

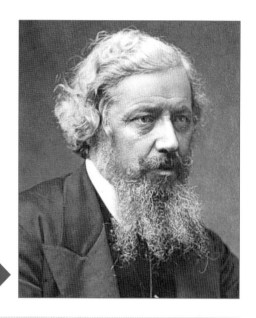

George Dawson

Corporation Street during the Coronation celebrations for King George VI in 1910

Gas Lighting, Corporation Street and Water from Wales

When Chamberlain became Mayor, Birmingham Corporation took over two private gas companies which had been overcharging customers. After ten years it had supplied 600,000 private lamps and 10,000 public lamps. The profit it made was used to improve other public services. In the same year, Chamberlain approved the demolition of streets of overcrowded housing close to New Street and Old Square. They were replaced by Corporation Street, a new road with shops, offices and law courts, but thousands of poor people were forced to leave their homes and find somewhere else to live. This was because the Corporation took no responsibility to rehouse those people. Chamberlain's grandest project was to bring fresh water to Birmingham. Huge reservoirs were built in the Elan Valley in Wales to supply water to the town. The scheme which began in 1894, cost £6,600,000 and was opened by King Edward VII in 1904. Birmingham people still drink high-quality soft water from Wales.

Chapter 14

WORKING WOMEN

Workers, Mothers and Housekeepers

Birmingham was not only created by men. Women worked in industry, ran businesses and set up their own clubs and societies. They led varied lives as workers, mothers and home keepers, and contributed many different skills to the development of Birmingham.

Female labour was needed for local trades. In workshops and at home, women and girls finished off buttons, metalware and guns, which had been manufactured by men. There was little education available for working women, but they managed households, raised children, cared for the sick and looked after the family income.

Italian women buying onions in the Wholesale Market, Moat Row

Working-class women doing the laundry

Local Businesswomen

Miss Florry (1744–1832) was one of the first local businesswomen. She was born in Ireland and came to Birmingham with her father in 1748. He failed as a businessman, but Miss Florry became a successful trader and employed male clerks and commercial travellers.

George Holyoake (1817–1906), who campaigned for improved rights for workers, described his mother's workshop for making horn buttons: 'She received the orders; made the purchases of materials; superintended the making of the goods; made out the accounts; and received the money; besides taking care of her growing family.'

Adverts for female-run businesses survive from the nineteenth century and reveal that women were manufacturing corsets and teaching dancing, shorthand and typewriting. A Birmingham directory from 1841 shows that about 800 businesses, 9% of the total in the city, were run by women. They were food sellers, shopkeepers, owners of laundries, a stone mason, gun makers and a steel-mill owner. Mary Anne Lloyd ran one such business. She managed the family brassworks for twenty years after the death of her husband in 1861.

Female Organisations

When it was formed in 1825 the Female Society for the Relief of British Negro Slaves was perhaps the first women's organisation in Birmingham. In the mid-nineteenth century a group of young females formed a very different society, the Birmingham Maidens' Club, where the members agreed to remain unmarried. The club had to close down after most of them abandoned their promise!

There were organisations created for women, as well as by women. The first school for wives, which taught home management and the avoidance of alcohol, was established in 1847. Richard Cadbury (1835–1899), the Quaker cocoa and chocolate manufacturer, set up the first crèche in the 1860s to care for his workers' children.

Working girls drinking tea at Gillott and Sons

Working-class women outside their homes

Votes for Women

The right to vote was a very important political issue at the time. The Female Political Union developed as an offshoot of the Birmingham Political Union, and it supported the campaign for the vote. Women joined trade unions and campaigned to obtain the vote for all adults. Nineteenth-century women could not vote in elections or become MPs, although they could be involved in local matters such as the management of schools.

The suffragette campaign in early twentieth-century Britain was set up to secure votes for women. In 1909 Prime Minister Asquith came to speak at Bingley Hall, where the ICC now stands. His speech was interrupted by women who climbed onto the roof to protest about his refusal to give women the vote. But it was not until 1918 that Parliament granted women the right to vote in national elections.

A Million People and New Industries

In 1901 Birmingham was home to 522,204 people and by 1938 its population had reached 1,048,000. This was partly because the boundaries of the city expanded to take in Harborne, Aston Manor, Erdington, Handsworth, Kings Norton and other villages. The population also grew because more workers moved to the city to work in industry. They made cycles, motorcycles, tyres, vinegar, sauces, tea, plastics, electrical goods and cars.

Women workers making hand grenades at the Mills Munitions Company during World War I

Herbert Austin: Popular Cars at Affordable Prices

Herbert Austin driving an Austin 7 in 1925

Herbert Austin (1866–1941) turned Birmingham into a centre for the manufacture of British motor cars. He was born in Buckinghamshire and came to Birmingham after going to Australia to work in engineering. In 1893 he was employed by the Wolseley Sheep Shearing Company, which made shearing machines, when its owner, Frederick Wolseley, asked him to run a branch of his business in Birmingham. Austin agreed and managed the branch successfully. He also designed cars for the firm, but in 1905 he left to set up his own business, the Austin Motor Company at Longbridge. In 1914 his company produced 1,500 cars a year and employed 2,000 workers.

During World War I (1914–1918) the firm made guns, trucks and aircraft, and by 1918 it employed 22,000 people. When the war ended, Austin looked for new designs to keep his factory going. In 1922 he created a small car, the Austin 7 or Baby Austin, which sold for £165. This was an affordable price for shopkeepers and well-paid office and factory workers. The factory at Longbridge continued to make cars for one hundred years after it was built, but now in 2005 its future is uncertain.

The Hall of Memory in Centenary Square was built to remember those who were killed in World War 1. This photograph shows the Hall with the Big Wheel in the background

World War I: Fighting Men and Working Women

148,000 local men joined the armed forces during World War I. About 11,000 of them were killed. Army service meant there were fewer men to work in those industries necessary for the war, so firms recruited women to make rifles, machine guns and grenades. They did well-paid, skilled work which had been denied to most of them before the war. Their wages gave them some independence from men. But when the war ended the men who returned home went back to their jobs. Factories stopped making weapons and women had to stop working in them.

Chinese Workers and Refugees

During the war local firms also employed Chinese men who had been sailors on British ships. John Beard, a British trade union official, feared that they would be paid low wages and therefore undercut the wages of British workers. Instead of trying to prevent their employment, he believed that the Chinese should work for the same wages as Englishmen. So Beard encouraged them to join unions to give them the same rights as other workers. After the war some of these workers stayed in Birmingham and ran their own Chinese laundries.

World War I began in Serbia in 1914 and Birmingham became home to refugee children who fled that country. They were looked after by Dame Elizabeth Cadbury who provided a home and education for them in Bournville. Local people also offered shelter, food and work for refugees from Belgium, where there was heavy fighting between German and British troops.

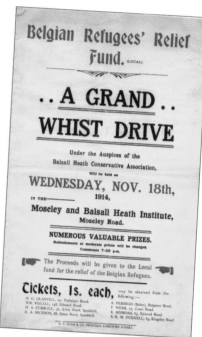

Poster to raise money for Belgian refugees, 1914

'War made us Fatherless': Children at a Co-op Rally in about 1920

Chapter 16

HOMES, HEALTH AND LEISURE

Workers at Cadbury's in Bournville, 1926

George Cadbury and the Bournville Estate

In 1878 George Cadbury (1839–1922), the brother of Richard Cadbury, built a new factory outside Birmingham in an area he called Bournville. The factory produced cocoa and chocolate. As a Quaker, Cadbury wanted to improve the conditions of workers and their families who lived in unhealthy and overcrowded back-to-back or terraced houses. In 1895 he started to build good-quality homes which had spacious gardens for growing vegetables.

In 1900 George Cadbury set up the Bournville Village Trust and gave it more land to build more homes. The Trust created parks, playgrounds and sports facilities, and built shops and a school. Because Quakers oppose the drinking of alcohol, no pubs were allowed on the Trust's land. There are still no pubs on the Bournville Estate today.

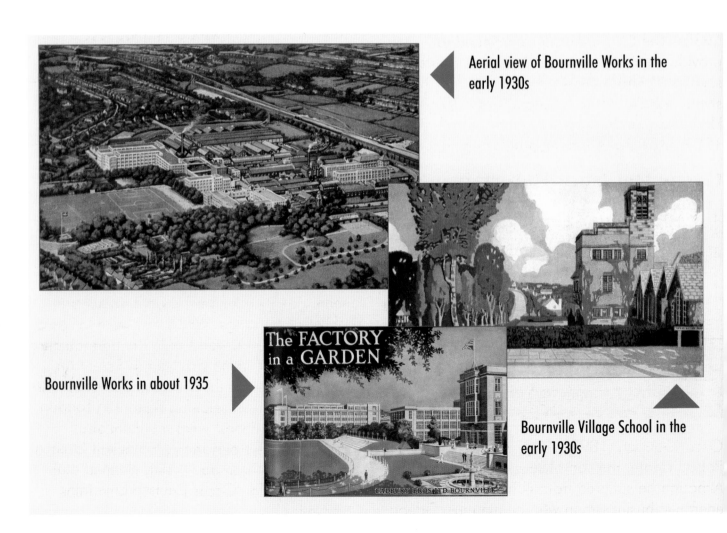

Aerial view of Bournville Works in the early 1930s

Bournville Works in about 1935

Bournville Village School in the early 1930s

Council Houses and Suburban Homes

Visitors came to Bournville from all over the world to see how a successful community could be created which linked industry, homes for workers and plenty of parks and gardens. But many workers could not afford to live in Bournville because rents were high. Birmingham's population continued to grow in the 1920s and 1930s, and more homes were needed. The local council built estates for industrial workers in Kingstanding and Lea Hall, and private companies built houses for office workers, managers and teachers in Quinton, Hall Green and outside the city in Sutton Coldfield and Solihull.

New council housing in Hurlingham Road, Kingstanding, in 1931

Work and Leisure

Birmingham was very lucky to escape the worst of the heavy unemployment which affected other parts of Britain, especially Northern England and South Wales, in the 1920s and 1930s. The city's industries continued to provide plenty of work. But in inner-city areas, such as Nechells and Ladywood, people lived in slums and did not have enough to eat. However, conditions did improve overall. By 1939 one third of Birmingham's population lived in homes that had been built after 1919. More people lived longer, fewer babies died before the age of one, working hours were reduced and wages increased. People had more free time to listen to the radio, read library books and newspapers, play sport, visit pubs, go to dance halls or see films. By 1938 there were ninety-eight cinemas in Birmingham. It cost one shilling (five pence) to see a film in the 1930s, and men and women with enough time and money might go several times a week.

Oscar Deutsch: Entertaining Our Nation

The Odeon Cinema, now a Bingo Hall, in Kings Road, Kingstanding

Oscar Deutsch (1893–1941) was born in Balsall Heath, the son of Jewish refugees. Although he suffered from ill health, he was an energetic businessman who created the Odeon cinema chain. The buildings were constructed in the latest Art Deco style and had the best equipment. His wife, Lily, designed the comfortable furnishings. They made sure that cinema goers no longer sat on hard seats in shabby surroundings. When they went to see a film they entered a world of luxury and fantasy. Deutsch's first cinema was built in Perry Barr, but he also created the most famous cinema in Britain, the Odeon Leicester Square in London. The original 'odeons' were amphitheatres where plays were performed in Ancient Greece. But Deutsch's clever advertising claimed that Odeon stood for 'Oscar Deutsch Entertains Our Nation'.

Chapter 17

WORLD WAR II

Evacuees from Birmingham in about 1941

Refugees and Soldiers from Overseas

When Hitler seized power in 1933 in Germany his Nazi government began the persecution of Jewish people and other minority groups. By 1939 thousands of Jews had fled to other countries and several hundred arrived in Birmingham. When war broke out the government was suspicious of people who had come from Germany and many Jews were arrested. Because Italy was a German ally this created problems for Italians already settled in Birmingham. Even though many of them had joined the British army, some were treated with suspicion, arrested and transported to the Isle of Man where they lived in camps.

When the war ended in 1945 some Jewish children whose parents had died in German concentration camps came to Birmingham. They then were adopted by local Jewish families who helped them to rebuild their lives.

People of many different nationalities fought for Britain as soldiers, sailors and airmen. After the war ex-servicemen from the Caribbean, India and Poland made their homes in Birmingham.

Air Raid Shelters and Allotments

In 1939 the residents of Birmingham feared that the city would be destroyed by German air raids. Large anti-aircraft guns were set up in parks to shoot down planes, and shelters were built in school playgrounds and back gardens to protect people from bombs. Children were evacuated to safe areas in the countryside where they stayed with other families. Most of these evacuee children returned after a short time away from home.

German U-boats sank many ships which were bringing food to the UK from overseas. This led to food shortages, so the government introduced ration books and vouchers for each person to ensure that everyone had enough to eat. Local parks were turned into fields for growing food and many schoolchildren spent their summer holidays digging up potatoes. The 'Dig for Victory' campaign urged ordinary people to grow vegetables in their gardens, and to rent allotments to produce beans, broccoli and tomatoes. There are still many allotments throughout Birmingham.

An instructor wearing a gas mask for practice rescue work during World War II

Shadow Factories and Spitfires

In 1939 Hitler attacked Poland, and Britain declared war on Germany. Throughout the late 1930s the government feared that war would break out and it had prepared for conflict. New buildings called 'shadow factories' were constructed next to existing factories. These made aircraft, tanks and guns. The best-known shadow factory was at Castle Bromwich. During the war it made 11,000 Spitfire fighter planes and 300 Lancaster bombers. These days the factory manufactures Jaguar cars.

Final assembly of the Spitfire at Castle Bromwich during World War II

World War II poster asking people to save their kitchen waste

Clearing up after a bombing raid, Small Heath, 1940

Birmingham and the Blitz

'Blitz' is the German word for lightning and it is used to describe the bombing attacks by German aircraft on British cities during the war. Between 1940 and 1943 there were 77 air raids on Birmingham. 2,241 people were killed, 12,391 houses were destroyed and 302 factories were damaged. The worst air raid was on the 19th and 20th November 1940 when 1,353 people were killed; 53 of them at the Birmingham Small Arms (BSA) rifle factory in Small Heath.

In December 1940 another air raid damaged St Thomas's Church. Only the bell tower survived. After the war it became part of St Thomas's Peace Garden, a memorial to people who died in the war and a reminder of the destruction that war brings.

When We Build Again

After the terrible experience of war, people wished for a better future and looked for ways to create a lasting peacetime. In 1941 the Bournville Village Trust produced a book about changing the city called *When We Build Again*. The book looked forward to a new Birmingham which would be carefully planned to provide wide roads, an unpolluted environment and spacious houses with gardens. These ideas influenced the planners who rebuilt the city after the war.

Aerial view of Spaghetti Junction

Suffolk Queensway, part of Birmingham's Inner Ring Road

Manzoni and the New Birmingham

Herbert Manzoni (1899–1972) was one of the urban planners. He was City Engineer and Surveyor from 1935 to 1963 and was responsible for many changes. Old homes were demolished and new council houses were built. In the 1960s the Bull Ring Shopping Centre was created and the Rotunda became a distinctive local landmark. Multi-storey car parks were constructed and subways allowed pedestrians to cross busy roads safely. New roads included the Inner Ring Road, Aston Expressway and Gravelly Hill Interchange or 'Spaghetti Junction', a loop of roads which linked Birmingham to the M6. When Spaghetti Junction opened in 1972 Birmingham became the hub of Britain's motorway network, just as it had been the heart of the canal system in the eighteenth century and of the railways in the nineteenth century.

Problems for Local People

Not everyone was impressed by the changes. Old buildings were destroyed and communities were uprooted. Some of the new tower blocks and council houses were cold and damp and had few facilities for children and older people.

Norman Power (1916–1993) was one local man who criticised these changes. He was born in Birmingham and after World War II he became vicar of St John's, Ladywood. In 1965 Power published *The Forgotten People*, a book which attacked how people in Ladywood were uprooted and moved without consultation during the slum clearances and rebuilding work of the 1950s and 1960s. He believed such schemes destroyed local communities: 'It is easy to see Birmingham's vast programme for central area redevelopment in terms of plans, buildings and sky-lines, and to overlook its effect on the lives of the people.'

In the 1960s Birmingham was a thriving city, but the 1970s and 1980s were difficult times. The motor car industry and manufacturing were in decline and there was less money to invest in the city. By the 1980s even the brand-new Bull Ring of the 1960s had become shabby. Local roads were blocked with traffic during the day and pedestrians were afraid of using subways as they were seen as dangerous and badly lit.

Tower block at Holloway Circus with the Chinese pagoda in the foreground

After the 1980s

Some good things came out of these problems. There was less money for large building schemes, but local people campaigned to preserve historic districts. Birmingham's Jewellery Quarter became a conservation area where old buildings were restored, cleaned and used for new purposes. Museums opened in the Jewellery Quarter, and at Soho House and Blakesley Hall. When the 1960s Bull Ring Centre was knocked down and then replaced in 2003, the new shopping district followed the street pattern of the old Birmingham market area. The past as well as the present became a source of pride for local citizens and a means of attracting visitors to the city.

The Rotunda, the Bullring and St Martin's Church

Chapter 19

NEW COMMUNITIES

Migrants and Refugees

In the twentieth century many people came from overseas to settle in Birmingham. They were refugees who had fled persecution in their own lands or economic migrants who had come to find work. Yemenis first arrived in the 1930s. After 1945 people from British India (which became India, Pakistan and Bangladesh), the Caribbean, Cyprus, Hong Kong, Ireland, Italy, Poland and Serbia also came to the city. East African Asians in the 1960s and 1970s escaped from Kenya and Uganda. During the 1980s Vietnamese 'boat people' left hardship in Vietnam to live in Birmingham. Refugees from Afghanistan, Bosnia, Iran, Iraq, Kosovo, Somalia and other African countries settled here in the 1990s. The 2001 census showed that one-third of Birmingham's residents described themselves as coming from a non-British background (see Appendix). This is one of the largest populations in the country, which makes Birmingham one of the most multi-cultural cities in Britain.

Inside of St Lazar's Serbian Orthodox Church, Bournville

The Islamia Alaquia Zawiya, the first mosque in Birmingham

Ceiling of St Lazar's

Racial Discrimination

Life was hard for those newcomers who faced hostility and racial discrimination. Signs outside some rented accommodation in the 1960s announced: 'No Blacks, no Dogs, no Irish'. Esmé Lancaster came from Jamaica to work as a teacher in 1950. She was offered a job at a local school, but on the day she was due to start, other members of staff refused to work with her because of the colour of her skin. So she decided to follow what became a successful career in

Sikh and English workers at Startins, Aston

child care and the probation service. When she retired, Esmé set up the Young Mothers' Relief Association to provide child care for working mothers. Esmé faced great difficulties in her early career, but in 2000 she received an MBE from the Queen for her community work.

Community Leaders

▲ Worshippers inside the Dar-Ul-Uloom Islamia Mosque, Golden Hillock Road

Many of the new settlers made a significant contribution to the life of the city and their own communities. These are just a few of them. In the 1940s Shaikh Muhammad Qassim al'Alawi, a Yemeni, set up the city's first mosque. Dr Dhani Prem became Birmingham's first Indian councillor in 1946 and he campaigned for improved health services and understanding between different nationalities. Henry Gunter from Jamaica campaigned in the 1950s to end discrimination against black workers on Birmingham's buses. Chaudhry Zaman Ali from Kashmir established a special burial ground for Muslims and ran the city's first halal slaughterhouse. In the 1980s a Catholic priest from Vietnam, Father Peter Dao Duc Diem, helped Vietnamese refugees set up home in Birmingham.

Alec Issigonis and the Mini

One famous incomer made a huge impact on the motor industry and the local economy by creating one of the great British cars. Alec Issigonis (1906–1988), born in Turkey, was fascinated by motor cars. During and after World War 1 his education was disrupted and he was forced to leave home, but this did not stop his ambition to be a car designer. He fled to Britain where he was able to study engineering. In 1955 Issigonis came to Longbridge to work for the British Motor Corporation. This new company had been created from the Austin and Morris firms. In the late 1950s Issigonis designed a car, the Mini, which was sporty, inexpensive and did not use much petrol. More than five million of these cars were produced between 1959 and 2000.

▲ Making the Austin Mini at Longbridge in 1963

Chapter 20

Rebuilding Again

Birmingham grew as a city because of industry and trade, but in the 1970s and 1980s factories and workshops closed down. The city was hit by heavy unemployment and thousands of local peole lost their jobs. In the 1990s

Aerial view of construction work at Brindley Place

Birmingham started to recover its prosperity and pride as new jobs were created in shopping, banking, scientific and medical research, tourism, entertainment and the arts. These changes have given the city a new skyline. In 1991 the International Convention Centre on Broad Street, a concert and conference venue, and the National Indoor Arena, a sports and entertainment complex, were opened. More recent projects have led to new buildings in Brindley Place, with its Sea Life Centre, offices, restaurants and luxury flats, the new Bullring for shopping, and Eastside, a creative, media and learning district close to Millennium Point. Outside the city centre, a huge housing estate was successfully rebuilt in Castle Vale.

The Arts and Entertainment

Changes in work and leisure have had a huge impact. Manufacturing remains a vital part of Birmingham's wealth, but tourism, sports and leisure have increased in importance. The city used to be famous for its industrialists, but people across Britain are more likely now to associate the city with Birmingham Royal Ballet, the City of Birmingham Symphony Orchestra, bands such as Led Zeppelin, UB40 and The Streets, writers such as Jonathan Coe and Benjamin Zephaniah, and Olympic stars such as Denise Lewis. Theatre, dance, sport, museums, film festivals and events such as the Muslim Eid and Sikh

Vaisakhi celebrations have become major attractions. The Ladypool Road in Sparkbrook is home to Birmingham's famous Balti houses and many Kashmiri restaurants.

Ladypool Road ▶

The five 'beloved ones' outside Birmingham Council House during the Sikh celebration of Vaisakhi in 1999

A City of Many Faiths

Since the 1960s office buildings and tower blocks have dominated Birmingham's skyline, but the landscape also contains spires, domes and minarets, which represent the different religions of the city. Out of a population of nearly a million, over half are Christians and a fifth are Muslims with substantial numbers of Sikhs and Hindus (see Appendix). Birmingham has over 650 churches for over forty Christian groups, about eighty mosques, several Sikh gurdwaras, Hindu and Buddhist temples and three synagogues. Birmingham has always been a place where individuals with different beliefs have settled. In the past Quakers, Jewish people and Catholics came to stay. Birmingham today is home to people from many different religious backgrounds.

A City of Many Changes

Throughout the centuries, people of diverse backgrounds, beliefs and races have lived and worked in Birmingham. Their lives have contributed to and shaped all the changes that have happened in the city – industrial growth, urban development, political reform and social change. In different ways they have created Birmingham's past and present. Today the city attracts people to work in the suburbs or the commercial centre near Colmore Row, shop in the Bullring or read and research in the Central Library. They can also make the most of the opportunities provided by schools, colleges and universities or enjoy the pubs, clubs, restaurants and cinemas around Broad Street or Hurst Street. Birmingham continues to flourish as one of the UK's most diverse cities – and its people thrive, work hard and enjoy their lives in this vibrant and busy place.

The Rotunda and the new Bullring at night

Appendices
FURTHER INVESTIGATION

Books, printed materials and original documents

The following are useful introductory books:

Berg, Jonathan, *Positively Birmingham* (Birmingham Picture Library, 1999)

Chinn, Carl, *Birmingham: Bibliography of a City, Birmingham* (The University of Birmingham Press, 2004). This is a guide to books about Birmingham.

Chinn, Carl, *Brum Undaunted: Birmingham During the Blitz* (Birmingham Libraries, 1996)

Dick, Malcolm, *Celebrating Sanctuary: Birmingham and the Refugee Experience 1750–2002* (Refugee Action, 2002)

Foster, Andy, *Birmingham* (Pevsner Architectural Guides, Yale University Press, 2005)

Grosvenor, Ian, Mclean, Rita and Roberts, Sian, *Making Connections: Birmingham Black International History* (Birmingham Libraries, Birmingham Museums and the University of Birmingham, 2002)

Hodder, Michael, *Birmingham: The Hidden History* (Tempus, 2004)

Leather, Peter, *A Brief History of Birmingham* (Brewin Books, 2001)

Leather, Peter, *A Guide to the Buildings of Birmingham* (Tempus, 2002)

McKenna, Joseph, *Birmingham: The Building of a City* (Tempus, 2005)

Upton, Chris, *A History of Birmingham* (Phillimore, 1997)

Local Studies and History on Floor 6 of Birmingham Central Library and Birmingham City Archives on Floor 7 hold a range of resources on the history of Birmingham, including photographs, maps, videos and magazines as well as books and documents.

Websites

Information and pictures about Birmingham history can be found by searching for subjects in a search engine. Some of the most useful individual websites are:

www.birmingham.gov.uk   www.digitalhandsworth.org.uk
www.revolutionaryplayers.org.uk   www.virtualbrum.co.uk

Places to Visit and Museums

There are lots of interesting places to visit in Birmingham. The Rabbit Guide to Birmingham (Clifton-on-Teme, Polperro Heritage Press, 2004) is a helpful guide. Information about museums can be found at www.birmingham.gov.uk The main museums in Birmingham are:

Aston Hall, Trinity Road, Aston. Tel: 0121 327 0062
Blakesley Hall, Blakesley Road, Yardley. Tel: 0121 464 2193
Sarehole Mill, Colebank Road, Hall Green. Tel: 0121 777 6612
Soho House Museum, Soho Avenue, Handsworth. Tel: 0121 554 9122
Birmingham Museum & Art Gallery, Chamberlain Square. Tel: 0121 303 2834
The Museum of the Jewellery Quarter, 75–79 Vyse Street, Hockley. Tel: 0121 554 3598
The Pen Room, The Argent Centre, Hockley. Tel: 0121 236 9834, www.penroom.co.uk

TABLES

The population figures before 1801 are estimates and different sources will provide alternative numbers. The figures after 1801 are based on census returns. There was no census in 1941 because of World War II. The charts for Religions and Ethnic Groups are taken from information in the 2001 census.

Population

YEAR	No. of people
1066	Less than 100
1300	1000
1500	1,500
1650	5,000
1700	8,000
1730	15,000
1750	24,000
1760	35,000
1785	52,000
1801	73,670
1811	85,753
1821	106,722
1831	146,986
1841	182,922
1851	232,638
1861	296,076
1871	343,787
1881	400,774
1891	478,113
1901	522,204
1911	840,202
1921	919,444
1931	1,002,603
1938	(estimate) 1,048,000
1951	1,112,685
1961	1,107,187
1971	1,014,670
1981	1,006,527
1991	961,041
2001	977,099

Religions

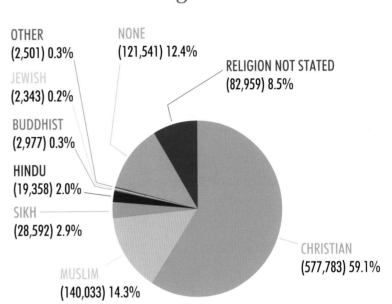

OTHER (2,501) 0.3%
NONE (121,541) 12.4%
RELIGION NOT STATED (82,959) 8.5%
JEWISH (2,343) 0.2%
BUDDHIST (2,977) 0.3%
HINDU (19,358) 2.0%
SIKH (28,592) 2.9%
CHRISTIAN (577,783) 59.1%
MUSLIM (140,033) 14.3%

Ethnic Groups

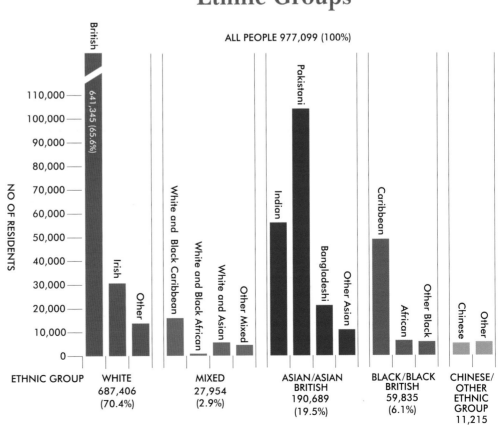

TIME CHART

Year	Events in Birmingham 700 to 1889	Events in British and World History
700	Rough date for establishment of an Anglo-Saxon settlement in Birmingham	Rough date for the coming of Christianity to communities in the West Midlands
1066		William I conquered England
1086	Birmingham was a tiny settlement owned by William Fitz Ansculf of Dudley	Domesday Book
1166	Peter de Birmingham established a market in Birmingham	
1539		Death of Guru Nanak, Founder of the Sikh Religion
1558		Elizabeth I became Queen 1558–1603
1635	Aston Hall built for the Holte Family	
1642		English Civil War 1642–1651
1643	Battle of Birmingham	
1725	St Philip's Church built, now Birmingham's Anglican Cathedral	
1742	Birmingham's first newspaper, Aris's Birmingham Gazette printed	
1756		The Seven Years War (1756–1763) increased demand for Birmingham's industrial goods
1765	Start of Lunar Society	
1769	First canal opened in Birmingham	
1789		French Revolution
1791	Priestley Riots	
1793		War with France (1793–1815) increased demand for locally made products
1796	Boulton and Watt's Soho Foundry opened to make steam engines	
1807		Slave Trade abolished in 1807
1832		The First Reform Act enabled electors in Birmingham to choose two MPs
1833		Law passed to abolish slavery in the British Empire
1837	Liverpool to Birmingham Railway opened	Victoria became Queen (1837–1901)
1851	Completion of St Chad's Roman Catholic Cathedral	
1856	Singers Hill Synagogue built	
1873	Joseph Chamberlain became Lord Mayor	
1874	Aston Villa Football Club formed	
1884		Parliament gave the right to vote to most men
1888		Football League set up

Year	Events in Birmingham 1889 to the Present	Events in British and World History
1889	Queen Victoria granted Birmingham city status	
1895	George Cadbury began building the Bournville Estate	
1904	Elan Valley scheme opened. It supplied fresh water to Birmingham from Wales	
1905	Herbert Austin set up the Austin Motor Company in Longbridge	
1914		World War 1 (1914–1918)
1928		All women over 21 obtained the right to vote
1935	Herbert Manzoni became Birmingham's Chief Engineer	
1939		World War Two 1939-1945
1940	Severe air raids killed many local people	Winston Churchill became Prime Minister
1941	First mosque in Birmingham opened	
1947		India achieved independence from Britain. India and Pakistan became independent countries
1952		Elizabeth II became Queen
1959	Production of the Austin Mini started	
1962		Jamaica achieved independence from Britain
1964	Bull Ring Centre opened	
1968	Completion of St Lazar's Serbian Orthodox Church, Bournville	
1971		Bangladesh became independent of Pakistan
1972	Spaghetti Junction opened	
1977	National Exhibition Centre opened	
1979		Margaret Thatcher elected Prime Minister until 1990
1982	Birmingham Central Mosque opened	
1991	International Convention Centre opened	
1997		Tony Blair became Prime Minister
2003	New Bullring opened	War in Iraq

INDEX